GEORGIA
impressions

photography by James Randklev

FARCOUNTRY
PRESS

Right: Ossabaw Island on Georgia's ninety miles of Atlantic Ocean coast.

Title page: In north Georgia's mountains, Cohutta Wilderness is part of the Chattahoochee National Forest.

Front cover: Spanish moss hangs from ancient live oaks on Cumberland Island.

Back cover: The Escowee River flows through rhododendron and mountain laurel forest in Chattahoochee National Forest.

ISBN: 1-56037-199-4
Photographs © by James Randklev unless otherwise indicated
© 2001 Farcountry Press

Created, produced, and designed in the United States.
Printed in Korea

Above: Cotton that has burst out of the boll is ready for picking.
ROBB HELFRICK PHOTO

Facing page: Dodd Creek in Raven Cliffs Wilderness Area, which straddles a few miles of the Appalachian Trail in north Georgia.

Above: One of the nation's oldest chartered colleges, University of Georgia at Athens dates from 1785.

Facing page: Georgia's pecan trees provide spring beauty, along with a famous cash crop.

Above: Helen reinvented itself as an alpine village and tourist destination in the 1970s after the local lumber industry failed.

Left: Heggies Rock in Columbia County's piedmont country is a Nature Conservancy Preserve.

Above: Seaside mosaic on Wassaw Island: sand dollars, shells, and a blue crab claw.

Facing page: Largest of the Sea Islands in the Atlantic Ocean, St. Simons serves up colonial history along with waterborne recreation.

Left: Swan House, Atlanta, dates from the 1920s, and offers public tours.

Above: Brotherton House in Chicamauga and Chattanooga National Military Park witnessed the seesawing Civil War battles here, and stands where the Union line was breached by Confederates.

14

Above: Kolomoki Mounds Historic Park, near Blakely, holds seven mounds built by area natives between 5000 B.C. and 1300 A.D.

Facing page: Longleaf pines grow amid cordgrass on Ossabaw Island.

Above: Peaches, state symbol of Georgia, are one of its greatest cash crops.

Left: Banks Lake National Wildlife Refuge in south Georgia offers camping, boating, fishing, nature trails, guided boat tours, and a museum.

Above: Godby Springs, near Lake Seminole in southwest Georgia.

Right: Toccoa Falls in northern Georgia, at 186 feet in height, is taller than Niagara Falls.

Above: Wisteria blooms in Providence Canyon State Park.

Left: Outside West Point, a major textile-production town.

Above: Okefenokee Swamp has been a wildlife refuge since 1937, and is home to cypress trees and waterlilies like these.

Facing page: The daintily stepping DeSoto Falls in Chattahoochee National Forest.

In 1902, Martha Berry began teaching school in a one-room log cabin in Rome; from this beginning grew today's Berry College with its oak-lined drives.

Above: In Savannah.

Facing page: Autumn touches Rock Town on Pigeon Mountain.

Above: Reindeer moss spreads its intricate lace.

Facing page: Shrimp boats along the Altamaha River near Darien.

Above: Fort King George State Historic Site, Darien, housed Scottish high-lander troops in the 1730s, sent to protect the young British colony.

Right: The Tallulah River is tamed by a dam except for parts of April and November, when it is allowed to return to whitewater status.

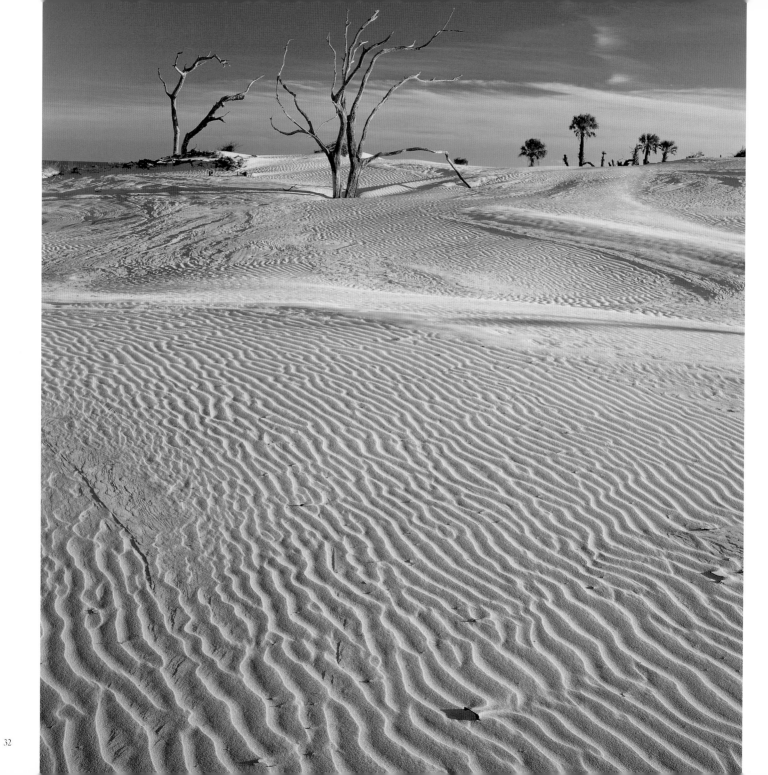

Above: The Georgia Capitol in Atlanta sports a dome covered with gold mined in the state.

Facing page: Skeleton and living trees rise among Cumberland Island sand dunes.

Above: Dogwood blossoms mean that spring has arrived.

Facing page: The Chattahoochee River and the Flint River form Lake Seminole, southwest Georgia's excellent fishing hole.

Above: Banks Lake, near Lakeland.

Right: Wormsloe Plantation at Savannah was begun by one of Georgia's original colonists and now is a historic site open to the public.

Water iris in Callaway Gardens resort near Pine Mountain.

Above: Watson Mill Bridge extends 229 feet across the South Fork River, and is the state's longest covered bridge still at its original site.

Facing page: Providence Canyon in its namesake state park was created by water flows resulting from 19th century farming practices.

Above: Lichen and pine cone still life.

Left: Live oaks in Cumberland Island National Seashore, which is kept pristine by limiting visitors to 300 per day.

Above: Day's end at the Mosquito River on Little Saint Simons Island.

Right: A leopard crab makes its way through a field of clam shells.

Above: Wild horses on Cumberland Island National Seashore are descended from herds the Spanish brought when they took over the island in 1566.

Facing page: A gull's-eye view of St. Catherines Island and the Atlantic Ocean.

Above: The coastal plain's Altamaha River is the largest unaltered river in the southeastern United States.

Facing page: Bull Sluice Rapids, Chattooga River.

Above: Once the private retreat of one of the nation's wealthiest families, Goodyear Cottage on Jekyll Island now serves the public.

Facing page: Goose Pond on Ossabaw Island is a good place for an alligator to take the afternoon sun.

Above: Spring sun lights up a hickory tree on Pine Mountain in Roosevelt State Park.

Facing page: Billy's Lake is one of sixty found within Okefenokee Swamp.

Above: Georgia's state flower is the Cherokee rose.

Facing page: This building at Pebble Hill Plantation, winter home for Northern industrialists, housed the horses.

Above: One way to enjoy Savannah is a paddlewheel steamer ride on the Savannah River.

Left: Unicoi Lake State Park offers hiking, boating, fishing, and swimming.

Above: Crescent House in Valdosta's historic district exhibits thirteen columns in honor of the original thirteen British colonies.

Facing page: Twisted old live oaks and palmetto share sandy land.

Above: Ocmulgee Lake, in its own state park, was created in 1940 with donated land and a dam across the Little Ocmulgee River.

Right: The Lapham-Patterson House at Thomasville shows the playful side of Victorian architecture.

Right: Clover and purple vetch go wild in Coffee County.

Below: Washington, Georgia, was founded in 1773 and named for General George Washington in 1780, while he still led American troops fighting the Revolutionary War—the first United States city to be named for him.

Above: Fort Frederica withstood would-be Spanish invaders of the British colony in 1742, but was leveled by fire only sixteen years later.

Left: Jekyll Island Club Hotel, the club house for a community of elaborate "cottages" when tycoons owned the entire island and jealously guarded their privacy, today is a public resort.

Above: Cloudland Canyon State Park in Georgia's extreme
northwestern corner, lives up to its romantic name

Facing page: Brasstown Bald, reaching 4,784 feet in elevation,
is the highest point in Georgia.

Left: The blackwater Ogeechee River rambles for 245 miles before meeting the Atlantic Ocean.

Below: Wood fern offers a cool geometric pattern.

Above: George T. Bagby State Park in southwest Georgia is a haven for conferences and vacations that include swimming, golf, tennis, boating, and hiking.

Right: Lake Conasauga in the Cohutta Wildlife Management Area.

Above: On St. Catherines Island, a sabal palm rises above marsh grasses.

Facing page: A golden autumn day along Johns Creek in the Cumberland Plateau.

Above: Stone Mountain holds the world's largest relief carving, which portrays Jefferson Davis, Robert E. Lee, and Thomas "Stonewall" Jackson.

Left: Bond Swamp National Wildlife Refuge, near Macon.

Above: Roswell, a small town just north of Atlanta, is home to Bulloch Hall, a mansion dating from 1839, where Theodore Roosevelt's parents (who also were Eleanor Roosevelt's grandparents) were married; today it is a museum.

Facing page: Cool off at Helton Creek Falls near Neels Gap in the Appalachians.

Sundown along the Brickhill River, Cumberland Island,
silhouettes live oak, Spanish moss, and palmetto.

JAMES RANDKLEV

Master landscape photographer James Randklev has photographed America for thirty years, primarily with a large-format camera that provides the rich images collected in this volume. His brilliant and sensitive work has made him one of the Sierra Club's most published photographers, and his color photographs have appeared in books, periodicals, and advertising—and have been exhibited in shows in the United States and abroad. In 1997, he was the sole American chosen to exhibit in the International Exhibition of Nature Photography in Evian, France. His previous book on the Peach State was *Georgia: Images of Wildness,* published in 1992.